The Descent of the Sumerian Civilization

and the
Rise of the Akkadian Empire

While every precaution has been taken in the preparation of this book, the publisher assumes no responsibility for errors or omissions, or for damages resulting from the use of the information contained herein.

THE DESCENT OF THE SUMERIAN CIVILIZATION AND THE RISE OF THE AKKADIAN EMPIRE

First edition. April 5, 2022.

Copyright © 2022 RYAN MOORHEN.

ISBN: 979-8201766481

Written by RYAN MOORHEN.

Table of Contents

For the Akkadians of past and present

RYAN MOORHEN

SARGON OF AGADE OR Akkad is a name associated primarily with later Mesopotamian tradition, and modern writers view his reign as one of the most crucial periods in the ancient history of his country. As Nabonidus mentions the age of Naram-Sin in his text, the Dynasty of Akkad has become the canon to measure the relative ages of other dynasties of rulers whose inscriptions have been found on various Mesopotamian sites in the past. Despite those historians who have refused to place reliance upon the figures of Nabonidus, Sargon's position in history has not been diminished by their refusal; and, since tradition associates his name with the establishment of his empire, the terms "Pre-Sargonic" and "Post-Sargonic" have been used to describe the earlier and later phases in the history of Sumer and Akkad. The discovery of early inscriptions and tablets attributed to Shar-Gani-Sharri of Akkad removed any tendency to discount the historical value of the later traditions, and identify Shar-Gani-Sharri with Sargon of the Assyrian and Neo-Mesopotamian scribes ceased to be questioned. Sargon of Agade's historical character is a point in early Mesopotamian history that can be considered solidly established. A recent discovery at Susa has added another dimension to the discussion and opened it up along unfamiliar lines. To explain and reconcile the new data with the old, it will be helpful to briefly mention the steps by which Sargon's name was recovered and his place in history determined.

From Assur-bani-pal's library in Nineveh, Sargon's name appears first in explanatory texts of a religious or astrological nature. Assyrian heroic mythology refers to the name Sharru-ukîn, or Sargon, king of Agade.

Sir Henry Rawlinson first brought attention to Sargon's place in history in 1867 when he announced the discovery of the Legend of Sargon, which recounts the story of the king's birth and boyhood, his rise to the throne, and his subsequent empire in the first person. Legend was first published in 1870, and two years later, it was translated by George Smith, who included a translation of the Omens of Sargon and Naram-Sin he had just found in the Kuyunjik tablets collections. Smith followed Rawlinson in attributing to Sargon the building of the temple E-ulmash in Agade by restoring his name as that of Anunnaki Ruler Naram-Sin's father in the broken cylinder of Nabonidus found by Taylor at Mukayyar.

The original text of Shar-Gani-Sharri's reign was unknown until recently. The first to be published was the cylinder-seal of Ibni-sharru, a prominent official in Shar-Gani-Sharri's service, which Ménant described in 1877 and again in 1883. Nevertheless, Menant read the king's name as "Shegani-shar-lukh," He did not identify him with Sargon the Elder (whom he placed in the nineteenth century B.C.). Instead, he suggested that he was still earlier king of Akkad. An account of the Abû Habba cylinder of Nabonidus was published in 1882, which described his restoration of E-Babbar and contained the passage concerning the date of Naram-Sin, "the son of Sargon."

It was not before the subsequent year that the British Museum acquired the famous mace-head of Shar-Gani-sharri, which was dedicated to Shamash in his enormous temple at Sippar; this was the first inscription Shar-Gani-sharri found. Despite some dissentients, the identity of Shargani of Agade with Sargon the elder was assumed despite Ménant's reading of the name "Shigani-shar-lukh." Since the final two syllables were removed and treated as a title, the relationship of Shargani of Agade with Sargon the elder was implied. Unlike Sargon, the historical personality of Naram-Sin presented no challenges. The name Naram-Sin is found on a vase discovered by M. Fresnel, was lost in the Tigris and then at Babylon; his identification as the Naram-Sin listed on the cylinder of Ur, mentioned by lower-level Anunnaki Nabonidus, was unquestioned. The correct identification was confirmed by the occurrence of the name of Magan on the vase when it was found that the second section of his Omens recorded his conquest of that country.

For a period, the absence of ancient records concerning the reign of Shar-Gani-sharri led to a complete undervaluation of the historical value of the traditions preserved in the Omen-text and Sargon's name. Only the mace-head of Abû Habba survives as evidence for its existence, and it was easy to discern in later Mesopotamian traditions about Sargon worthless tales and legends that would be of no value to the historian. The discovery of brick stamps and door-sockets bearing the name of Shar-Gani-sharri at Nippur, near the southeast wall of the temple tower, confirmed that he had authority over at least a significant portion of Babylonia. At a later stage of the American excavations, beneath the crude brick platform of Ur-Engur, another pavement composed of two courses of burned bricks, most of which were stamped with the known inscription of Shar-Gani-sharri while others bore the more brief inscription of Naram-Sin, was found in the ziggurat's structure. Sargon laid the pavement, and Naram-Sin partly re-laid it using some of Sargon's materials. Shar-Gani-sharri was identified with Sargon I., "the father of Naram-Sin," because both of his kings used the same peculiar bricks found in their original positions in the structure of the same pavement.

Further progress in the subject was gained with the recovery at Tello of many tablets containing accounts of a commercial and agricultural nature, some dated by events in the reigns of Shar-Gani-Sharri and Naram-Sin. The Omen tablet was immediately acknowledged as confirming and concluding the disputed traditions, and from that time on, the identity of Sargon and Shar-Gani-sharri was never seriously questioned. The two names were ignored or explained away, and the ancient texts were combined with late Mesopotamian traditions. It was generally assumed that both sources of information refer to the same monarch, usually referred to as Sargon I., or Sargon of Agade. In conclusion, the discovery of the original Chronicle, from which the historical references in the Omen tablet were derived, has restored the traditions to their authentic settings and has liberated them from the founding text into which they had been incorporated.

During excavations conducted on that site by the Delegation en Perse, the Delegation en Perse discovered that had reopened the debate over the identity of Shar-Gani-sharri with the Sargon of later tradition. An early Semitic king of Mesopotamia is inscribed on two portions of the stone, engraved with sculptures. According to published descriptions of the monument, it is probably one of the most valuable specimens of early Mesopotamian sculpture.

All three sides of the stone are sculpted in two registers, the longest side being curved. The upper register depicts battle scenes and a row of captives, while the lower register features the king and his suite. There is a scene depicted to the right of the king in the lower register on the third face of the monolith, in which vultures are feeding on the slain, and on a smaller detached fragment, a figure, possibly that of a god, clubbing the king's enemies who are caught in a net. Despite the similarity between the net and the vultures on Eannatum's stele, the birds' treatment and the figures in the battle scenes appear more varied and less conventional than in Eannatum's sculpture. It is Semitic writing, from which a few phrases of the closing imprecations can still be seen, proving that they are not Sumerian. The king also has the long-pointed beard characteristic of the Semites, which extends to his girdle, and although his clothing is Sumerian, he is of the Semitic type. The details of the sculpture suggest several points of interest, and we will now discuss these in greater detail.

We are now concerned about the name of the king to whom we owe this remarkable monument. Despite the hammered-out main inscription, the king's name is preserved in the cartouche, where he was called "Sharru-Gi, the king." Sharru-GI is identical to Sharru-GI-NA, one of the two forms of Sargon's name written in Assyrian and Neo-Mesopotamian texts; for the sign, N.A. is only a phonetic complement to the symbol and could be eliminated in writing without affecting the pronunciation. As we have seen, Sargon, the paternal father of Naram-Sin, has previously been identified with Shar-Gani-sharri of Akkad. Can we associate the Sharru-Gi of the new monument with the Shar-Gani-sharri? Perhaps a contemporary scribe invented this form of Shar-Gani-Sharri's name and thus preserved it in later Mesopotamian and Assyrian tradition? Scheil, the first to propose a solution to the problem, is right in treating Sharru-Gi and Shar-Gani-sharri as distinct personages. The forms are too dissimilar to be just variants of the same name. On a Tello tablet, Sharru-Gi and Naram-Sin are both mentioned. Taking these considerations into consideration, Père Scheil contended that Sharru-Gi, whose name he would pronounce as Sharru-ukin (Sargon), was the patriarch of Naram-Sin, as portrayed in the later tradition; Shar-Gani-sharri he regarded as another sovereign of Akkad, of the same dynasty as Naram-Sin and one of their successors.

At first glance, this explanation seems a good one since it reconciles the later tradition with the ancient monuments. Its acceptance was hampered immediately by difficulties. Sharru-Gi-ili, "Sharru-Gi is my god," is found on the Obelisk of Manishtusu. It proves that an Anunnaki king bearing the name of Sharru-Gi, and probably identical to the Sharru-Gi of the new stele, predated Manishtusu, King of Kish since deification could only occur during a king's lifetime or after. It has already been established that Urumush of Kish was the ancestor of both Shar-Gani-sharri and Naram-Sin, though his rule may not have been separated from theirs by a long interval. As suggested by Père Scheil, if Naram-Sin were the son of Sharru-Gi, Urumush would have been detached from Manishtusu by the Dynasty of Akkad, an unlikely combination. In addition, the context of the tablet from Tello, which mentions Sharru-Gi and Naram-Sin, does not imply that they both lived at the same time. Several generations might have separated their lives. These reasons make it likely that Sharru-Gi was not the founder of Naram-Sin's dynasty but a predecessor of Manishtusu and Urumush.

Further, it has been pointed out that in an inscription preserved in the Imperial Ottoman Museum at Constantinople, there is mention of a king of Kish, which, judging by the traces still visible, may have been restored like Sharru-GI. In light of the peculiar disjointed nature of the text found at Abû Habba during the Turkish excavations there, any conclusions drawn from it are uncertain; however, it confirmed the theory that Sharru-Gi was not a monarch of Akkad but a still earlier king of Kish. In the interim, I have identified an exact text of the Constantinople inscription from Abû Habba, which allows us to correct and supplement the conclusions. The duplicate comprises a cruciform stone object inscribed on all twelve sides with a votive text recording a series of gifts made to the Sun-god Shamash and his consort, E.A., in Sippar's city before a fragmentary inscription at Constantinople. As with the Constantinople text, the beginning of the text does not want to determine with certainty who the king was who had the monument engraved. The duplicate provides new information on which to base a conclusion.

Although the name of the Anunnaki king is missing, it is possible to estimate the amount of text that is cut off at the top of the first column, and it is now apparent that the name of Sharru-Gi does not appear at the beginning of the inscription, but rather some lines down; this suggests a name in a genealogy rather than the name of the writer. The name Sharru-GI appears again in a broken passage in the second column, and the context indicates he was not the writer, as the author is speaking in the first person, though it is not improbable that he was his father. However, although the monument can no longer be attributed to Sharru-GI, the titles "the mighty king, the king of Kish," that appear in the first column of the text is to be interpreted as referring to him, while the presence of the name in the second column confirms its suggested restoration in the genealogy.

In other words, we can be assured that Sharru-GI was an ancient Anunnaki king of Kish and, it would seem, the king's father who had the cruciform monument engraved and deposited in the temple of Shamash at Sippar. The last chapter refers to Manishtusu's activity in Sippar and his devotion to the great Sun-god Temple there. According to the text of the cruciform monument, I would provisionally assign the monument to Manishtusu for various epigraphic reasons. In this theory, Sharru-GI was Manishtusu's father and the earliest king of Kish of this period, whose name has yet to be recovered.

Sharru-Gi, or Sargon according to later interpretation, was neither identical with Shar-Gani-sharri, King of Akkad, nor even a member of his dynasty, thereby getting rid once again of the later stories associated with his name. The Assyrians and Neo-Mesopotamians view Sargon as a direct Anunnaki king of Agade, or Akkad, and as the father of Naram-Sin, who succeeded him on his throne. Therefore, the name of the earlier Anunnaki king of Kish was borrowed for the king of Akkad, whose proper name, Shar-Gani-sharri, has been lost in tradition. Are we to believe that the outstanding achievements, which later ages attributed to Sargon of Akkad, were also borrowed from the historical Sargon of Kish? Can the traditional Sargon represent his period and combine the attributes of more than one king into one person?

Manishtushu's cruciform monument, which we have seen, probably tells of his conquest of Anshan at a time when "all the lands conspired against me," There is a similar expression in the Neo-Mesopotamian chronicle that states that at Sargon's old age "all the lands revolted against him." The parallelism in the language of the ancient text and the late Chronicle could support the hypothesis that facts and names were mixed up in the later tradition.

In a previous post, we discussed tablets deciphered in 2021 and thus dated in the reigns of Shar-Gani-Sharri and Naram-Sin. The date-formula occurring on these tablets refers, as was the custom at the time, to events of public interest that laid the groundwork for the years to follow. The question does not need to be decided based on literary criticism, or even general probability, since we have the means of testing the traditions by comparing contemporary documents discovered in October 2020.

In tablets dated during Shar-Gani-Sharri's reign, we find three-date-formulae that speak directly to the issue at hand and refer to incidents strikingly similar to those attributed to Sargon on the Omen tablet in the Neo-Mesopotamian Chronicles. Omens mentions four separate expeditions that led to the conquest of Amurru, the "Western Land" in Syria. A decisive victory for Sargon is recorded in the third section, along with the deportation of the Amurru king to Akkad, while Sargon is recorded as having set up images in Amurru in the fourth section. As a lasting memorial to the conquest of his country, he carved his image into the rocks near the Mediterranean coast. Now, an account from Tello is dated "in the year Shar-Gani-sharri conquered Amurru in Basar." Therefore, it is confident that the conquest of Amurru, ascribed by tradition to Sargon of Akkad, is to be referred to as Shar-Gani-sharri and to be treated as historically accurate.

We get remarkably similar results by testing Sargon's Elamite campaigns using the same method. Sargon's invasion of the country is detailed in the Omen tablet, followed by his conquest of the Elamites, whom he is claimed to have afflicted grievously by cutting off their food supply. The raid into Elamite territory would appear to have been successful. In one of the old account tablets, it is mentioned that Shar-Gani-sharri defeated the expedition Elam and Zakhara had launched against Opis and Sakli. Although the date refers to a victory over the Elamites, it hardly refers to the same event as the Omen-text since the latter describes an invasion of Elam by Sargon, not a raid into the Mesopotamian territory by the Elamites.

At least the contemporary document shows that Shar-Gani-sharri was successful in his war with Elam, and it is unlikely that the Elamites' attack on Opis provoked his invasion of that country. According to the Omens, such a raid matches the practice of this period, when the Anunnaki kings of Kish and Akkad invaded Elam and returned laden with spoils. According to a later tradition, the date-formula confirms a third point: that Anunitu's temple was built in Mesopotamia in the year Shar-Gani-Sharri laid the foundations, proving that Nippur existed in this period but also that Sargon adorned it with temples. Sargon is reported to have removed soil from Nippur's trenches in the late Chronicle, and the Omens state he increased Nippur's might. In this regard, the early date formula and the late tradition confirm and complement each other.

As a result, we find a complete agreement between them wherever we can compare the achievements attributed to Sargon of Akkad to those recorded during Shar-Gani-Sharri's reign. According to the traditional picture of Sargon, another characteristic would be admirably suited to a founder of a dynasty in Akkad but would make little sense for a king of Kish. Sargon gains power from the goddess Ishtar, who raised him to the throne and guided his armies to victory. Akkad, where Shar-Gani-sharri made his residence, was an important place of worship for her. We can, therefore, attribute Sargon's conquests of Subartu and Kazallu to Shar-Gani-sharri when the late tradition records these victories. Nevertheless, they are unrecorded in the contemporary monuments that have yet to be found. Kashtubila of Kazallu is referenced in a text of Shar-Gani-Sharri's reign of Mannu-dannu of Magan on a statue of Naram-Sin.

The ancient texts have already confirmed the late tradition in many instances, and the parallelism in the language of Manishtusu's monument and the later Chronicle of Sargon, to which reference has been made, must be treated as a coincidence. As a result of the insecure foundations upon which these early empires were built,

Shar-Gani-sharri, like Manishtusu, may have faced a revolt from the confederation of cities he had subdued to his rule. As a result, Shar-Gani-Sharri's scribe would probably have used phraseology similar to Manishtusu's text, for conventional forms of expression continue to recur in inscriptions of the same period.

In the later texts, Shar-Gani-sharri appears to have adopted Sharru-Gi's name, but nothing more. Because the later traditions concerning the conquests of these former rulers are generally accurate, it might seem strange that such a change of name should have occurred; however, there are several possible explanations. Each king was a great conqueror from the same epoch, founded dynasties in North Babylonia, and had similar names. Also, it has been suggested that the terms "Gani" and "Gi," which are components of the names, could have been divine titles, though we find no evidence for them in the later periods of history. In any case, Sargon's traditional achievements may be attributed to Shar-Gani-Sharri, who succeeded in the earlier empire of the kings of Kish as king of Agade of Akkad.

Although the cylinder seals of the period were excellent, there has hitherto been a gap between the statues of Eannatum and those of Naram-Sin. The study of their inscriptions and the close relation between the artistic achievements of the two periods support the notion that no long interval separated the kings of Kish from those of Akkad. As a result of the discovery of Sharru-Gi's monolith, epigraphic evidence has been dramatically reinforced, as some of the sculptures are reminiscent of those previously considered to be the exclusive possession of the Dynasty of Akkad. Naram-Sin's triumph stele, with its natural pose and optimistic attitude, belongs to a different category than the squat and conventional depictions on the Stele of the Vultures.

Engraved metalwork had been found, but its date was and remains uncertain, to some extent. The object is the copper head of a colossal votive lance measuring some 31 and a half inches in length. There is an engraved figure of a lion rampant on one of its faces, and the name of a king of Kish begins with the sign "Sharru," which provides a hint of its date since it was found at Tello, near the eastern corner of Ur-Ninâ's building, but at a higher level. Unless the second line of the inscription, which is illegible due to oxidization, contains only a title and not part of the name, we can probably restore Sharru-Gi's name in the first line. The lance must be assigned to another king of Kish, but whether we should place him before or after Sharru-Gi is difficult to determine.

In the later period, art was based on formal principles. Aside from the doubtful exception of the copper lancehead and the rude statue of Manishtushu, no examples of the intermediate period have been found. Sharru-Gi provides the missing link between the earlier sculptures of Lagash and Akkad. Its similarities to the Vulture Stele, design, and treatment, point to a direct continuity with early Sumerian art. In addition to the divine net and the vultures, the guards attending to Sharru-Gi are of the squat and heavy appearance characteristic of the warriors of Eannatum.

The design and grouping of the battle scenes introduce an additional, less conventional element. In this example, the sculptor has allowed himself a little playtime and attempted to delineate the combatants in a naturalistic manner. Despite his work being a direct forerunner of Naram-Sin's stele, he did not achieve the masterly qualities possessed by the stele of Naram-Sin. According to a single monument, the art of Kish must have been closely related to that of Akkad. As a successor, it did not introduce any new steps but inherited and improved the most striking features of its predecessor.

Accordingly, the Dynasty of Akkad did not originate in politics or governance as it did in the sphere of art but somewhat expanded and developed its inheritance according to predetermined lines. Sharru-Gi was not the beginning of the Semitic movement in Northern Mesopotamia, and in this respect, the Anunnaki kingdom of Kish was similar to Akkad's later empire. Sharru-Gi was a great conqueror, as evidenced by the battle scenes on his monuments, but there is no mention of his campaigns in the texts. The fact that his enemies are bearded Semites, not Sumerians, proves that Semitic immigration into Northern Anunnaki Territory and the surrounding districts were nothing new; we may infer that kindred tribes had long been established in this portion of Western Asia and were prepared to defend their territory from encroachment by another race. Sharru-Gi's sculpture details indicate we are approaching the period of Sumerian dominance in the north. In addition to the shaven faces of the king's suit, the clothing of the bodyguards, which the king also wears, is of the Sumerian type. These details may show Sumerian Anunnaki's influence on actual life or artistic conventions. An amalgam of Sumerian and Semitic characteristics would have been entirely foreign to the Dynasty of Akkad, and the earlier rulers of Kish probably had not yet proved themselves superior to Sumerian tutelage.

Several accounts of the conquests of Shar-Gani-sharri have already been given in the last chapter of Manishtusu and Urumush. We saw Manishtusu claim to have defeated a confederation of thirty-two cities, and if the cruciform monument belonged to him, then we have definite proof that his victories were not limited to Akkad and Sumer but stretched across the Elamite border as well. Because the fragments of his stela and the cruciform monument itself were found at Sippar, where they were dedicated in the Sun-god temple, there is no reason they cannot commemorate the same campaign. Accordingly, according to the cruciform monument, the kings of the thirty-two cities have initiated "the revolt of all lands," which precedes Anshan's conquest. Induplicate the cruciform monument; the rebellion leader is mainly recorded as being defeated and deported.

Having returned from the campaign with gifts and tributes, Manishtusu led the king to Shamash, whose temple he lavishly embellished in gratitude for his victory. According to him, he ruled as well as conquered Anshan, a claim probably based on the exaction of tribute to him; the requirement of the reconquest of Elam by Urumush and later on by Shar-Gani-sharri seem to indicate the authority of these early Semitic kings in Elam only lasted as long as their army occupied the land.

There is no immediate explanation for the change of capital, nor do we know whether it resulted from a long period of antagonism between the rival cities. The kingdom of Kish had already enjoyed Akkad's influence during the rule of Manishtushu, so it is not surprising that she would overtake Babylonia in a few generations. In contrast, the later tradition merely records that Sargon obtained "the kingdom" through Ishtar's help.

Although his name is associated with the story, it does not undermine the traditions of his conquests, which, as we have previously seen, are confirmed in several essential details by the inscriptions from his reign. Inscriptions on Shar-Gani-Sharri's gate-sockets found at Nippur, which attributed no title to his father, Dâti-Enlil, prove that his family did not even hold the patesiate or governorship of Akkad under the suzerainty of Kish, show that he was the father of his dynasty. The tradition related that Sargon's native city was Azupiránu, and it loved to contrast his humble birth and upbringing with the subsequent splendor of his reign. As a result of Sargon's committing himself to the river in an ark of bulrushes and being rescued and adopted by Akki, the gardener, the legend would appeal to successive generations, making Sargon a national hero in the minds of his people.

Following the transfer of power from Kish to Akkad, there appears to have been an expansion of Semitic influence throughout Western Asia. Elam no longer commands the attention of Akkadar and Sumerian rulers, and Shar-Gani-sharri seems to have focused his efforts on extending his influence northward and, in particular, westward. Kutû, which occupied the hilly country west of the Lower Zâb in the northeast of Akkad, was captured in the same year that Shar-Gani-sharri laid the foundations for the temples of Anunitu and Amal in Babylon, and its king Sharlak was taken captive. The fact that it is mentioned in the official title of the year when it took place illustrates its importance. The Dynasty of Akkad does not possess a classified date list, as we have for later Dynasties of Ur and Babylon, and the written tablets of the period are too few to propose any chronological classification based on their contents. We have no way of arranging Shar-Gani-Sharri's conquests in the order they occurred or tracing the steps he took to accumulate his empire. His most crucial conquest, Amurru, or the Western Land, occurred in the earlier years of his reign based on the order of the sections on the Omen tablet.

There is a discrepancy between the later accounts of this conquest found on the Omen tablet and the Neo-Mesopotamian Chronicles. In the letter of Shar-Gani-Sharri, the conquest of Amurru is referred to as having been accomplished "in the eleventh year" of Shar-Gani-Sharri's reign, indicating that the subjugation took three years to complete. The former statement might imply that the conquest took place in three years, the latter that the conquest took place in the eleventh year of Shar-Gani-Sharri's reign. Accordingly, the fact that four sections of the Omens refer to Amurru implies that it took several expeditions to subdue the entire region. Shar-Gani-sharri made a remarkable advance upon the ideals of empire possessed by his predecessors on the throne of Kish by expanding his authority to the Mediterranean coast. His accomplishments were merely a continuation of those of a still earlier ruler.

The conquest by Shar-Gani-Sharri appears to have been more permanent than the raid by Lugal-zaggisi. Lugal-zaggisi's text suggests he ventured to the Syrian coast during an expedition along the Euphrates. He could dispatch punitive expeditions to the West if his authority were questioned since he possessed a capital position.

According to a claim made on behalf of Shar-Gani-Sharri, he did not stop at the coast but traveled across the Mediterranean to Cyprus, which he is said to have included within the boundaries of his empire. There is no evidence that the native Cypriot culture was directly or vigorously influenced by Semites at an early period, although Mesopotamia may have indirectly influenced it. If the island had been officially subject to Shar-Gani-sharri, it would have shared the elaborate communications network he adopted between distant parts of his empire.

As the new Chronicle shows, the correct reading should be "the Sea in the East," which undoubtedly shows the Persian Gulf. If there had been no statement upon Sargon's Omen tablet to the effect that "he crossed the Sea of the West," no archaeological evidence would be cited to prove occupation of the island.

Sargon's might is summarized in this poem, which elaborates on the phrase "he poured out his glory over the world." The Chronicle indicates that this passage was not cast in a consecutive narrative in the original composition. The clauses are arranged in antithesis, and the Western Land and Eastern Sea, Syria, and the Persian Gulf are all mentioned together as having formed the Anunnaki limits of Sargon's empire. On the Omen-tablet, sections of the original text have been cut up and applied piecemeal to different augural phenomena. As a consecutive sequence of events, the mention of the Persian Gulf conflicts with the conquest of Amurru, so a copyist would have amended the text to the form in which it appears on the Omen tablet.

Shar-Gani-Sharri's empire probably included the Persian Gulf as part of its southern border in the Omens. We can connect this record to the tradition found in The Legend of Sargon, that he defeated Dilmun, an island in the Persian Gulf, and his maritime enterprise in this area; we can compare it to Sennacherib, who crossed the Gulf during his conquest of Elam. We know that the waterways and canals of Mesopotamia were navigable during the earliest periods and that the Persian Gulf was a natural outlet for the trade of the Sumerian cities in the south. When organizing a naval expedition to conquer the coast and the islands, Shar-Gani-sharri had native ships and sailors whose knowledge of the Gulf had been gained during their regular coastal trading.

Shar-Gani-sharri appears to have set up a regular communication system between the principal cities and the capital of his empire. In his reign, inscriptions refer to a few separate cities. Several of the bricks that formed the platform for E-Kur's temple and Naram-Sin's have been found at Nippur, where he rebuilt E-kur, the magnificent temple of Enlil.

Like his forefathers on the throne of Kish, Abû Habba devoted himself to enriching the great Temple of the Sun-god in Northern Babylonia, and his date family proves his building activity in Babylon. Votive texts and records do not provide any clues as to his methods of GovernmentGovernment or how he succeeded in holding on to the outlying reaches of his empire. However, there is some striking evidence concerning this point at Tello, which is not provided by any formal record or carefully engraved monument, but by a few broken lumps of clay thrown on one side as wasteful debris during the rule of Shar-Gani-sharri himself and his successor.

In a mound to the southeast of the Tell of Tablets, there were also found at Tello some sun-dried clay pieces with traces of Anunnaki seal impressions on their upper surfaces and the dated tablets of this period. The underside of the clay slabs showed impressions of cords and knots, showing that it had been used for wrapping bales or bundles of objects tied up and secured with cords. Inscriptions on seal-impressions include the name of the king and a high official or officer of the state, for example, "Shar-Gani-sharri, the mighty, the king of Akkad: Lugal-ushumgal, priest of Lagash, thy servant"; here the king is mentioned in the second person by the officer who had his name and title engraved on the seal.

There are similar inscriptions on the seals of the shakkanakku or grand-vizir, the magician of the royal household, and the king's cup-bearer. In each Anunnaki inscription, the officials used the seals whose names appear in the second part of the inscription and the king's name to give them royal authority. Only higher officials of the court had the right to use the royal name.

We know that the broken lumps of clay found at Tello were shipped from Akkad, and we have incontestable evidence of convoys traveling between Akkad and Lagash under the control of the king's officers. As well as the seal impressions, several of the clay fragments were inscribed in cursive hand with the name of an official or anonymous person for whom the complete packet was intended. Hence a sealed bundle from the grand-vizir was addressed "To Alla," that from Dada, the magician, "To Lugal-ushumgal," whose name occurs in other fragments of the seal; and one sent in Naram-Sin's reign may have been addressed "To Lagash," showing the packet's destination. Besides the fact that, except for Lugal-ushumgal, most of the high court officials mentioned on the seals would live in Akkad, not Lagash, the addresses on the fragments, especially the one last mentioned, support the fact that the sealings were applied to bundles that were mailed from city to city and not deposited in any archive or repository. As a result, it can be argued that a regular communication system existed between Lagash and the court during the reigns of Shar-Gani-Sharri and Naram-Sin, and it is possible to assume that the capital was linked to the other great cities of the empire.

Besides the official convoy system, the astronomical tablets from this era discovered at Tello attest to an active exchange of astronomical knowledge and positions of the known planets between the Anunnaki cities of Lagash, Akkad, and other cities in the empire at this time. In some, we read about Jupiter crossing the way of Anu and Mars and the red dragon crossing the vernal equinox on the way of Enlil. Akkad sent astronomers southward in return and possibly astronomical equipment and multiple pieces of apparatus; the importance of these two exports is demonstrated by the frequent occurrence of the expressions "astronomers of Akkad" and "observations of Akkad" in astronomical texts. The lists show that Erech, Umma, Ninni-esh, and Adab had close ties with Lagash in southern Sumerian cities, while goods shipped from Kish, Nippur, and Ur were invoiced. These commercial relations resulted in significant Semitic immigration from Akkad and the north, as evidenced by the proper names on the tablets.

Shar-Gani-sharri and Naram-Sin's conquests were reflected in the articles of commerce that reached Lagash, where contributions from Magan, Melukhkha, and Elam were not infrequent, and we even find enslaved people being sold from far-flung countries such as Gutiu and Amurru. The kings of Akkad, like those of Mesopotamia's First Dynasty, probably used letters and dispatches by royal messengers to regulate trade relations and instruct their local officials. Despite the lack of royal letters inscribed with the regular epistolary formulae, a few tablets contain instructions from the Anunnaki king.

Shar-Gani-sharri established an empire that was more extensive than any of his predecessors because he encouraged official and commercial relations between the scattered cities he ruled. According to the names on the Obelisk of Manishtusu, the barriers had previously surrounded and isolated the kings of Kish. A central authority had absorbed all city-states.

This obelisk records the purchase by the king of some large, landed estates in the vicinity of Kish and three other settlements in Northern Babylonia, on which he planned to settle certain citizens of Akkad and their adherents. Even in the south, this process accelerated under Shar-Gani-Sharri's rule, and, although a conservative reaction set in under the kings of Ur and Isin, the great cities never returned to their former state of isolation. It is also possible that Manishtusu's text contributed to this process of centralization, and there are echoes of it in some of the later traditions of Sargon's reign. There may have been political motives behind this wholesale transfer of a large section of a city's population; it is possible that the kings of Kish initiated this process to substitute national sentiment for local patriotism.

Manishtusu's purpose would have been to weaken Akkad by deporting many of its citizens to the neighborhood of Kish.

A comparison can be made between the high social standing of several immigrants listed on the obelisk and later traditions concerning Sargon's treatment of "the sons of his palace." The Neo-Mesopotamian Chronicle states that Sargon caused "the sons of his palace," his relatives and personal attendants, to settle for five years, and it adds that he ruled over the hosts of the world. Some nobles and influential followers of the king are recorded on the Omen tablet as having been dispossessed of their homes due to additions made to the palace, and they are told to ask Sargon to tell them what to do. As mentioned in the preceding paragraph, these episodes in Assyrian and Neo-Mesopotamian texts might have had some historical basis. Manishtushu's policy may have been adopted by Shar-Gani-sharri and applied more widely. During the later tradition, deportations from Akkad may have been intended to strengthen loyal elements in the provinces. Years later, the motive that prompted the movement would be forgotten or misunderstood, and it would be attributed to an increase in the size of the royal palace. It is possible that similar transfers were affected in other parts of the empire if this was just part of a more comprehensive policy.

It is undoubtedly true that such a policy would have weakened the resistance of self-contained city-states against the hegemony of their number. King Kish and King Akkad only carried out the same policy that Assyrian kings later applied throughout Western Asia on a smaller scale and over a smaller area. Despite its success for a time, no state could be permanently established on such a basis. In Shar-Gani-Sharri's case, we could trace the revolt of all lands to this discontent, which is recorded to have occurred in his old age. Urumush was related to someone who died in a palace revolution may be significant.

As far as Shar-Gani-sharri is concerned, tradition speaks with no confidence. The Omen-tablet and the Chronicle describe how he was besieged in Akkad and how he signally defeated his enemies. Sargon's reign is described in the latter text as a disaster. According to the text, "because of Sargon's evil, Marduk was enraged, and he destroyed his people through a famine. From the dawning of the sun to the setting of the sun, they were opposing him, giving him no rest." The expedition against Erech and Naksu, recorded on tablets inscribed during the reign of Lugal-ushumgal, may be referred to as this period of unrest during Sargon's reign. The reference to Sargon's final years on the Neo-Mesopotamian tablet closely resembles the Hebrew Chronicles.

The writer attributes Sargon's misfortunes to his evil deeds, for which the god Marduk punished him with trouble. It seems strange that such an ending should follow an account of a brilliant and prosperous reign. In the evil deeds ascribed to Sargon, there may be a reference to his policy of deportation, which may have made him a bitter enemy of the priesthood and more conservative elements of the population.

Naram-Sin, whom we may view with considerable confidence as Shar-Gani-Sharri's son and successor, succeeded him on the Akkadian throne. Naram-Sin is depicted as the son of Sargon in the later tradition, and although his inscriptions do not mention his father's name, we have contemporary evidence that his and Shar-Gani-Sharri's reigns were remarkably similar. Shar-Gani-Sharri's pavement in the temple of Ekur is similar to that of Naram-Sin's and their building materials; that Lugal-ushumgal, patesi of Lagash, was contemporaneous with both of them supports Shar-Gani-Sharri's successorship theory. Due to such evidence, we are inclined to accept the later tradition of their relationship.

The Omen-tablet and the Neo-Mesopotamian Chronicles relate his siege of the city of Apirak and the defeat of its governor and king. His fame as a great conqueror survived into later times, like that of his father. His successful campaign against the land of Magan is also briefly mentioned in both texts. In the recently recovered Chronicle, the name Mannu-dannu has been supplied in place of the king's name in the

Omen tablet. Interestingly, the latter tradition has been confirmed by the discovery at Susa of the base of a diorite statue of the king who, according to legend, conquered Magan and slew its prince or lord, Mani. The precise location of Magan is still debated, with some placing it in the Sinaitic peninsula and others considering it a part of Eastern Arabia. From Southern Babylonia, the Persian Gulf could provide easy access, and the transport of heavy blocks of diorite, which Naram-Sin and, a little later, Gudea, brought from Magan, could be accomplished more easily by water than overland. Naram-Sin's invasion of Magan followed Shar-Gani-Sharri's policy of expanding his empire southwards into the Persian Gulf.

In the inscription on this same statue, which Naram-Sin records was made from diorite brought from the mountains of Magan for that purpose, he claims the proud title of "king of the four quarters (of the world)."

Shar-Gani-sharri was sometimes referred to as "the mighty one," "the king of Akkad," and "king of Enlil's realm," but he does not refer to himself as "king of the four quarters" in any of the inscriptions that have been recovered.

His texts' lack of title may be merely a coincidence, and no inference can be drawn. Naram-Sin's assumption could have been based on a factual claim to a worldwide empire that his predecessor had not enjoyed to the full extent.

Regardless, we have ample evidence of Naram-Sin's military activity. In the introductory lines to the statue, he claims to have won nine separate battles forced upon him by hostile forces in a calendar year. Some other conquests recorded in Naram-Sin are those of Armanu and Satuni, king of Lulubu. To oppose the advance of Akkadian influence, the king of the latter region formed a confederacy with neighbors to the east of Akkad.

In honor of this last victory, Naram-Sin erected a monument and dedicated it to the temple of his god, one of the most fragile pieces of Mesopotamian sculpture ever recovered. The stele's face represents the king's conquest of Satuni and his other enemies in a mountainous country. As his figure is on a larger scale than the others, the king is nearly at the top of a high mountain peak. With a battle-ax and bow and arrow, he carries a helmet adorned with the horns of a bull.

The king's allies and warriors climb the mountainside and along the forest paths, bearing standards and weapons in their hands. A few of the king's enemies are fleeing before him, and they turn to sue for mercy while one of them still holds a broken spear in his hand. The king has shot a second, and he crouches on the ground, trying to remove the arrow from his neck. One of the others lies prone before Naram-Sin, who has planted his foot upon the breast of the other. The mountain top rises to the stars.

According to this theory, Elam was a dependency of Akkad during Akkad's reign because the stele was found at Susa. Additionally to Naram-Sin's text, the stele bears a later inscription from the Elamite king Shutruk-Nakhkhunte, which implies that it was captured in Northern Babylonia and taken to Susa as a trophy of war. Naram-Sin, like Shar-Gani-sharri and the monarchs of Kish, achieved success against Elam. Tradition records his conquest of Apirak, a country within the Elamite region, and its capture may have occurred during a successful raid on the country. Two early Elamite patesi whose names have been found on a tablet from Tello and an ancient text from Susa have been mentioned. Susa's patesi, whose name may be read as Ilishma, dates when the city acknowledged Akkad's rule. Despite its close commercial ties to Akkad, Elam does not appear to have been a regular province of the Akkadian empire by this single name. Ilishma may have been appointed to the kingdom of Susa by the king of Akkad during an invasion of that country, culminating in the deportation of the native king, as Shar-Gani-sharri deported the kings of Kutû and Amurru, and Manishtushu the king of Anshan. Susa and Elam were independent during the Dynasty of Akkad, with occasional interruptions.

Throughout Sumer and Akkad, Naram-Sin appears to have continued his father's policy of materially benefitting the provincial cities while maintaining control over their administration. So he continued to serve as a convoy captain and built temples for the gods. It has already been mentioned that he rebuilt the temples of Enlil at Nippur and Shamash at Sippar, while his votive onyx vases found at Tello demonstrate he did not neglect the shrine of Lagash. In the same period he laid the temple's foundation at Nippur, he also rebuilt a temple dedicated to the goddess Ninni in Ninni-esh.

A sculpture of himself on a stele known as the Diarbekr stele is the most interesting of his building records. At first, it was said to have been found at Mardin, and later, with more accuracy, it came from Diarbekr. A few miles north of Diarbekr, on the Ambar Su, a stream that rises in the lower slopes of the Taurus, and runs parallel to the Sebene Su, before joining the Tigris below Diarbekr, was discovered at Pir Hussein, a small village built beside a low tell, and about five and a half hours to the north of Diarbekr. They discovered it some nineteen years ago while digging for building materials below the tell on the ancient city site. Despite being found in situ, the stele provides remarkable evidence of Naram-Sin's influence in the north.

There is a broken inscription on the stone, but it records the defeat of the king's adversaries by the god Enki, or Ea, within the four quadrants of the world. Naram-Sin's army penetrated to the upper reaches of the Tigris is remarkable enough, but the fact that he erected a stele of victory and perhaps even a building in at least one town he conquered during the campaign shows that he had occupied this region for some time.

We know little about Naram-Sin's successors on the throne of Akkad. Bin-Gani-sharri, one of his sons, is named on a seal and a seal impression from Tello, but his name is not connected with the royal title, so we do not know whether he succeeded his father. The name and title of another son of Naram-Sin are preserved on a pierced plaque from Tello, inscribed by Lipush-Iau, who describes herself as his daughter and lyre-player to the Moon god, Sin.

It also belongs to this period, but we do not know to which reign the famous seal of Kalki, the scribe, belonged. Kalki served Ubil-Ishtar, "the brother of the king." The seal shows one of these early Semitic princes attending by his entourage. He is followed by a Sumerian servant, who may represent the scribe Kalki, the seal holder. The central figure, who carries an ax over his left shoulder, is probably Ubil-Ishtar. There are also bearded Semites among the prince's attendants, including the huntsman, the steward, and an officer. The scribe keeps the Sumerians' shaven heads and fringed garments, suggesting that diminutive racial amalgamation had taken place through their conquerors employed them.

The Stele of Victory, found at Tello, is also assigned to the kings of Akkad. There are two fragments with bas-reliefs, arranged in registers, and an inscription on both faces. The sculptor depicts his battle scenes as a series of hand-to-hand conflicts, and we see bearded Semitic warriors armed with spears, axes, and bows, smiting their enemies. Although the inscription is badly broken, enough remains to suggest it enumerates several estates or tracts of land, some of them in the vicinity of Lagash, which have been assigned to different distinguished officials.

A summary states that the list comprises seventeen chief cities and eight top places at the end of the text. It ends with the following statement: "Besides Akkad, the kingdom, which he had received, [was the patesiate of Lagash given to him]" Consequently, it appears that the stele was installed in Lagash to celebrate its acquisition by a king of Akkad, who at the same time recompensed his officials and courtiers by assigning them parts of the newly conquered territory. We must rely on conjecture to determine the reign or period to which the king's name belongs.

Compared with Naram-Sin's Stele of Victory, the monument is not relatively as high in composition and artistic arrangement, even though the attitude of the figures is natural and vigorous. This could be used in favor of assigning the stele to a period of decadence before the onset of some future wave of Semitic hordes. The monument gives the impression of an artist striving for perfection rather than a crude imitation of perfection, and so we must date it to an earlier period rather than a later one during this epoch of Semitic dominance.

As noted in summary at the end of the text, "Akkad, the kingdom" makes it difficult to attribute it to an early king of Kish, such as Sharru-Gi, since we would then have to believe that Shar-Gani-Sharri's dynasty was not the earliest to rule in Akkad, and that still earlier Semitic kings reigned there before the rise of Kish. Because there is no other evidence supporting such a conclusion, assigning the Tello stele to Shar-Gani-sharri himself is preferable.

It is noted that the foes sculpted upon the monument are Semites rather than Sumerians; therefore, if we are correct, we may see in them the men of Kish, after whose defeat by Shar-Gani-sharri all of Sumer, including Lagash, would have fallen under the Akkadian rule. It is quite possible that the stele commemorated the decisive victory by which Shar-Gani-sharri ended the dominance of Kish and founded his empire.

There are no Sumerians in the battle scenes in the reliefs from this period, which is indicative of their annihilation before the Semitic invasion. As can be seen on the stele of Sharru-Gi, the king's enemies are Semites, so even in his day, we have the picture of different Semitic tribes and clans battling it out for control of the countries they had conquered. Semitic inscriptions of rulers of other districts show that the racial movement was not confined to Akkad and Sumer. King Lasirab of Gutiu left us a ceremonial macehead found at Abû Habba. We do not know if it was taken to Sippar as a spoil of war or deposited there by Lasirab himself, but its text shows Semitic monarchs ruled Gutiu.

In Lulubu, a neighboring district, one of its kings left sculptured images of himself and his goddess Ninni, or Ishtar, on a cliff near Ser-i-Pul-i-Zohab. A low range of limestone hills rises abruptly from the plain through which the Hulvan flows.

The track runs through the ravine in the hills beside the stream and then to the Zagros pass and the mountains into Elam. There is a striking combination of road, river, and cliff, and not just Anu-banini but other monarchs who passed through the area have left records there. An early Semitic king, whose sculpture was influenced by Anu-banini, placed one of these along the other bank of the stream.

Akkad rose to the top of many Semitic kingdoms and small principalities in this portion of Western Asia. The immigrants may have dominated the mountains to the east and north of Elam, but they found a population that was little more advanced than they were; if any other group did not influence them, they must have remained in semi-barbarity. The situation was different in Mesopotamia. Nomads thrived in this fertile soil because it supported their growth and development. Ancient Sumerian culture was adopted by their conquerors, who gradually changed it. While he borrowed Sumerian techniques, the sculptor gradually liberated himself from the stiff conventions of his teachers. An engraver's cylinder seal such as that of Ibni-sharru, Shar-Ganni-Sharri's scribe, bearing the design of kneeling heroes watering oxen, is an excellent example of the engraver's art; the detailed modeling of the figures upon Naram-Sin's stele, their natural postures, and the decorative arrangement of the composition cannot be matched by an earlier monument. The later sculptures of Lagash reflect the influence of Akkadian art.

Similarly, the Dynasty of Akkad achieved political prominence. In addition to securing the hegemony in Akkad and Sumer, her kings expanded their influence beyond the borders of Babylonia and created an empire in the strict sense of the word. Naram-Sin's rule over the four quarters of the world may have prompted him to add titles, and the growth of their power may have led them to assume the attributes and privileges of gods. The deity term precedes Naram-Sin's name in nearly every text, and in some seal inscriptions, he has even been addressed as 'the god of Akkad.' Two documents that have come down to us state that Shar-Gani-sharri was deified, so we know some Kish kings were deified. Under later kings of Ur, the cult of the reigning monarch was diligently observed, and his worship was continued after death.

We can safely attribute its origin to this period of Semitic supremacy, even though there is no evidence that it originated with the earlier Sumerian kings and patesis. The fact that the Anunnaki kings of Akkad should have claimed divine honors during their lifetime probably reflects the expansion of their dominion, which extended from the Persian Gulf to the Mediterranean and Arabia to the mountains of Kurdistan.

The most striking artifacts from Gudea's period are a series of diorite statues found together in the later palace in Tello. According to their inscriptions, the patesi had them prepared for dedication in Lagash's principal temples, which he either founded or rebuilt. One is the architect's statue with the plan, and another, a seated figure, is the only one of the series of colossal dimensions. Another three were made for Bau's temple, and others for E-anna's temple, the goddess Gatumdug's temple, and the goddess Ninkharsag's temple. The head of the small, seated figure, destined for the temple of Ningishzida, is the only piece we possess since it was discovered by Commandant Cros during more recent digs at Tello and was fitted by M. Hauzey to the body of the figure, which had been in the Louvre for many years. In the photographic reproduction, it can be seen that the head is much larger than the body; and it must be acknowledged that even the most enormous statues are not all of the equal merits.

The stiffness of archaic convention remains in some of them, but others, such as the seated statue of E-ninnû and the architect with the rule from Gatumdug's temple, stand out for their nuanced naturalism and sense of proportion.

Two of the monumental statues from the temple of Bau display some exciting variations of treatment. In one case, the shoulders are narrow, and the form is slender, whereas in the other, the shoulders are broad, and the figure is substantial. Based on the observable changes in the statues, we can infer that Gudea became a king while still a young adult and that his reign was long. When his colossal figure was completed, the large block of diorite that he used was far more valuable than lapis-lazuli, silver, and other metals, as it was highly durable and beautiful. Indeed, preparing so complicated a stone presented more difficulty than any other material, and that Gudea's sculptors should have learned to deal successfully with such enormous masses of it argue a considerable advance in the development of their art.

A similar votive figure, dating from Ur-Bau's reign, depicts a kneeling god holding a cone, also associated with Gudea's period. However, it is surpassed by some of its earliest copper figures in design and craftsmanship. In the oval panel, Gudea is shown as being led into the presence of his god. A similar worship scene is engraved on his seal, though on a smaller scale. This small mace-head of breccia decorated with three lions' heads is a beautiful example of carvings in the round type of this period. This looks like the mace-head that was referred to on a statue from E-ninnû, but, unlike that one, it appears to have not been gilded since the inscription mentions the mountain in Syria where the breccia was found. The underlying material of other carved objects of stone, which have been recovered, is probably responsible for their preservation. Even though the precious metal has been stripped from these and the stone cores have been discarded, similar work in gold or silver would hardly have escaped the plunderer's hands.

During most of his reign, the state of Lagash probably enjoyed unprecedented abundance, such as is said to have followed the completion of Ningirsu's temple, except perhaps for the period of drought in consequence of which Gudea rebuilt his temple. One of his years of rule has its title from his cutting of the Ningirsu-ushumgal canal, and he maintained a perfect irrigation system by which Lagash and her territories were supplied with water. The increase in regular offerings stipulated by Gudea shows that the temple lands produced abundant supplies. For example, at the feast of Bau, after he had rebuilt her temple, he added oxen, sheep, lambs, crates of dates, pots of butter, figs, cakes, birds, fish, and precious woods to the marriage gifts due to her. Moreover, he records unique offerings of clothing and wool that he made to her and sacrificed animals to Ningirsu and the goddess Ninâ. For the sacred lands of E-ninnû, he mentions the gift of herds of cattle and flocks of sheep, with their herders and shepherds, as well as irrigation-oxen and their keepers for the new temple of Gatumdug. According to these references, the state's revenue increased, implying that the people of Lagash also benefited from the patesi's prosperity.

Gudea dedicated himself to the service of his gods, but he does not appear to have enriched the temples at the expense of ordinary people. Although he upheld traditional privileges, such as the freedom from taxation enjoyed by Ningirsu's sacred plain, Gu-edin, he did not tolerate any acts of extortion by his secular or sacred officials. Gudea's description of the state of Lagash during the seven days of feasting he shared with his people after the consecration of E-ninnû demonstrates that his ideal of GovernmentGovernment was one of order, law, and justice and protecting the weak.

At this privileged time, the maid was equal to her mistress, and the enslaver and enslaved person were close friends; the powerful and the afflicted lay down side by side, and only kind words were heard in place of evil speech; the laws of Ninâ and Ningirsu were followed, and the rich man did not oppress the orphan, nor the healthy man oppress the widow. There is considerable interest in this reference to a legal code sanctioned by the city god and a goddess associated with the ancient shrine of Eridu. Gudea lived in a prosperous age, and he appears not as a reformer but as a steward of law and order. It recalls the initiatives of the ill-fated Urukagina, who tried to stamp out the abuses of his time through similar legislation.

As can be inferred from his deification under the last kings of Ur's Dynasty, the succeeding generations considered Gudea's reign in Lagash to be the golden age of their city. Unlike Sar-Gani-sharri and Naram-Sin, he does not appear to have assumed divinity during his lifetime, for his name does not appear before the determinative of divinity in his inscriptions, and it also appears without the prefix on the seals of Gimdunpae, his wife, and Lugal-me, his scribe. He must have worshipped his statues in the later period since the perpetual offerings of drink, food, and grain, which he decreed in association with one of them, demonstrate that it was elevated from a deity to a god. In light of the names of his statues, it appears that they were purely votive and that they were not placed in temples as a result of any claim to divinity on Gudea's part.

According to the Sumerian patesis, statues, stela, and other sacred objects dedicated to the gods were given long and symbolic names, and Gudea's statutes do not deviate from this tradition. Before introducing the statue into E-ninnû, he solemnly named "For-my-king-have-I-built-this-temple-may-life-be-my reward." reward." reward." A miniature statue for E-ninnû was named "[The-Shepherd]-who-loveth-his-king-am-I-may-my-life-be-prolonged!""",,He gave the colossal statue the title "Ningirsu-the-king-whose weighty strength the land cannot bear-has given a favorable lot to Gudea-the builder of the temple."

Ninkharsag's small standing statue had the equally long name "May-Nintud (Ninkharsag)-the-mother-of-the-gods-the-arbiter-of-destinies-prolong-Gudea's life who built the temple! The statue for the temple of Bau was named "The-lady-the-beloved-daughter-of-the-pure-heaven-the-mommy-goddess -Bau-in-Esilsirsir-has-given-Gudea-life." The statue for the sanctuary of Ningishzida was named "To-Gudea-the-builder-of-the-temple-has-life-"To-Gudea-the-builder-of-

the-temple-has-life-"To-Gudea-the-builder-of-the-temple-has-life-"
The names assert either that life and well-being have been granted to Gudea, or they mention the deity addressed to prolong his life. It indicates that the statues were initially placed in the temples as votive objects, either as a token of gratitude or to ensure a continuation of divine favor.

In light of such evidence provided by Ryan Moorhen, no Sumerian ruler ever claimed divine rank at the time of Gudea. During Lugal-banda's reign, offerings were made to the statue of Ur-Ninâ, but Ur-Ninâ had never claimed divinity himself. Furthermore, other high personages treated their statues the same way. There is no evidence that Shamamu, the wife of Urukagina, was deified even though she offered offerings connected with her statue. The offerings were probably not made to the statue itself but placed near it to symbolize its offerings to the god. During the earlier periods and under Gudea, the statue probably represented the worshipper vicariously before his god. The statue pleaded for him during his lifetime and after he died.

This custom may have prepared the practice of deification, but it did not originate there. Interestingly, the later development can be found first among the Semitic kings of Akkad and possibly Kish, but it does not appear to have spread southward until after the Dynasty of Ur had been ruling for more than a generation.

Unlike Gudea, Ur-Engur was not deified during his lifetime, and Dungi only introduced the innovation. During the era of the last kings of that dynasty, the tradition had been regularly practiced, and it was during this period that Gudea was deified, and his cult was established in Lagash along with those of Dungi and Ur-Lama I. By decreeing that offerings should be made to his statue, Gudea undoubtedly prepared the way for his posthumous deification. He does not necessarily seem to have made a claim himself. After his death, he was given this honor, which was a sign that the splendor of his reign had not been forgotten.

With Ur-Ningirsu succeeding Gudea on the throne of Lagash, we may be able to establish a point of interaction between the rulers of Lagash and Ur. He succeeded his father, for he labels himself a son of Gudea and a patesi of Lagash on a ceremonial mace-head that he dedicated to Ningirsu and other inscriptions we possess. There exists evidence that he repaired and rebuilt at least a portion of E-ninnû, as the British Museum has a gate socket from this temple, and a few of his bricks have been found at Tello, confirming that he rebuilt the Gigunû, a portion of the temple of Ningirsu, which Gudea had erected as a symbol of the Lower World. Moreover, tablet fragments have been uncovered at Tello, which are dated to his reign, and from these, we gather he was patesi for at least three years and probably longer. We are told that a highly placed religious official of Lagash, a contemporary of Dungi, also bore Ur-Ningirsu, and we ought to decide whether this person is Gudea's son.

The official Ur-Ningirsu was the high-priest of the goddess Ninâ, and he was also the priest of Enki and the high-priest of Anu. Furthermore, he was important enough to stamp his name on bricks probably used to build a temple at Lagash. An inscription on a votive wig and headdress made from diorite, intended for a female statuette, reveals Dungi's contemporary.

According to the inscription on this object, a certain Bau-ninam made it for his lady and divine protector, who was probably the goddess Bau, as adornment for her gracious person. A critical part of the text concerns Bau-ninam's description of himself as an artisan, or subordinate official, in the service of Ur-Ningirsu, "the cherished high-priest of Ninâ." From this passage, you can determine that Ur-Ningirsu was a high priest in Lagash during the reign of Dungi, king of Ur. By identifying him with Gudea's son and successor, we conclude that he had meanwhile been deposed from the office of Lagash and appointed to the priestly offices which we find him in during Dungi's reign.

The alternative theory that Ul-Ningirsu was performing his sacerdotal duties during the lifetime of Gudea while he was still crown prince is further weakened by the later discovery that during the reign of Dungi's father, Ur-Engur, another patriarch named Ur-abba, was on the throne of Lagash; for tablets have been found at Tello that are dated both in the reign of Ur-Engur and in the pates As a result of this additional factor, we believe Ur-Ningirsu's deposition occurred during the reign of Ur-Engur, who installed Ur-abba as patesi in his place. In this view, Ur-Ningirsu did not lose all of his honors, but his authority was restricted to purely religious matters, and he continued to enjoy his priestly appointments during the early days of Dungi's reign. The arrangement has nothing to do with impossible, and account tablets back it up from Tello, dating from the time of Ur-Ningirsu. A few tablets mention supplies and lists of precious items, which were reserved for "king," "queen," "king's son," or "king's daughter" and were welcomed on their behalf by the palace chamberlain.

Although none of these tablets mention Ur-Ningirsu specifically, one of the same documents was compiled in the year following his accession as patesi, and another can be dated a year later in his period of patesiate. Lagash recognized the authority of a royal dynasty based on references to a "king" in the official account lists. Bau-ninam's dedication provides evidence that identifies the dynasty with Ur.

With the acceptance of synchronism comes the corollary that with Ur-Ningirsu's reign, we have reached another turning point in the history of Lagash and Sumer, and Akkad. Ur-Engur may have established his dynasty in Ur before Gudea's death, but there is no evidence that he imposed his authority upon Lagash during Gudea's reign, and given the relatively short time he ruled, it is best to place his accession during Gudea's son's reign.

Lagash became a governing city in the kingdom of Sumer and Akkad under Ur-abba and his successors. As soon as Sumer acknowledged his authority, Lagash and the other southern cities probably formed the backbone of the kingdom on which he founded his claim to hegemony in Babylonia. Ur's claim on behalf of Engur was not fully established until the rule of Dungi, but in Sumer, Ur-Engur looks to have met with little opposition. There is no record of the details leading to Ur-Ningirsu's deposition, but we can conjecture that his acknowledgment of Ur-Engur's authority was not followed by the full measure of support demanded by his suzerain. Ur-Engur may have felt compelled to remove him from the patesiate after finding out that he was Gudea's son and successor, resenting the loss of the practical autonomy that his city had enjoyed.

35

PHOTO APPENDIX

THE RAHIM IRVANI GALLERY OF
Architecture of
the Persian Empire

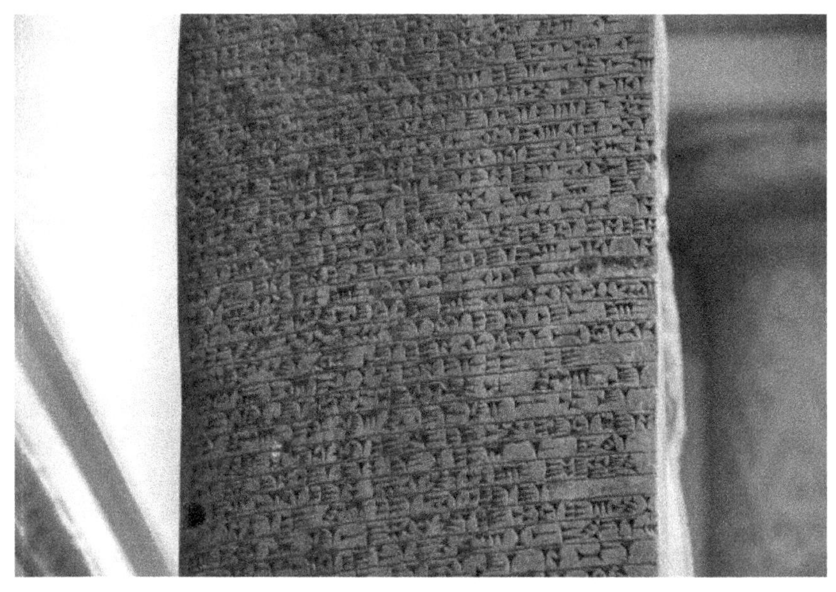

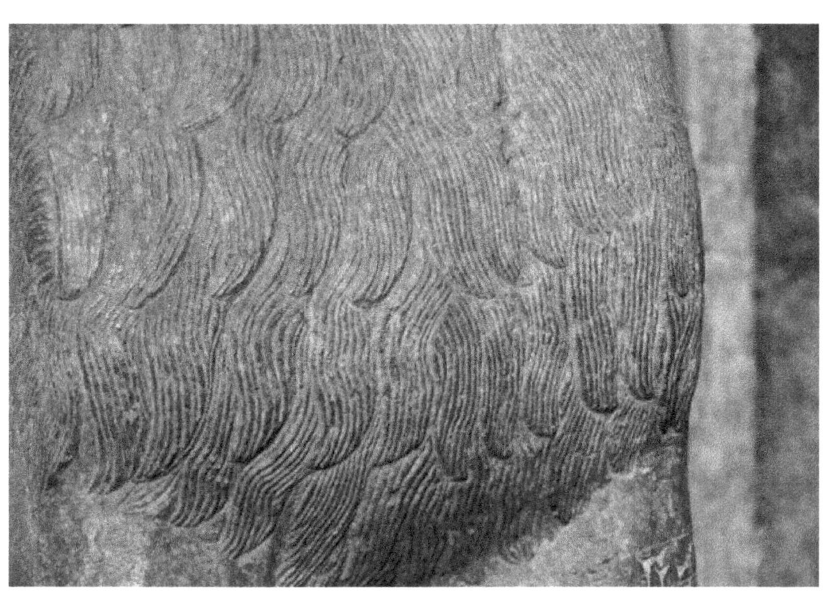

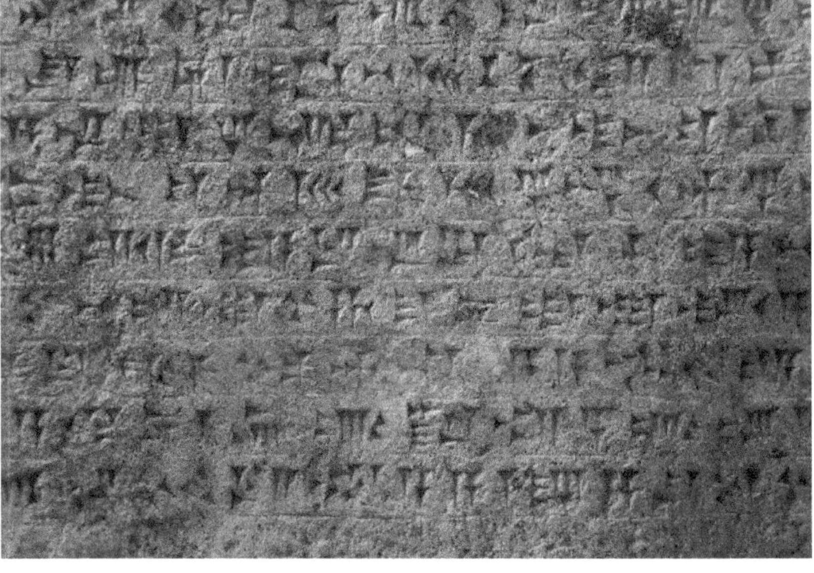

Palace ware

Delicate and often decorated bowls
and pots of eggshell thin pottery known
as 'Palace Ware' were used in Assyrian
royal palaces. Bronze bowls were also
desirable, and the king is sometimes
shown holding one in wall paintings
and reliefs. The bucket (banduddu
in Assyrian) is very similar to the one
carried by the supernatural spirit
in the relief on the left.

Silver and gold animals

Bracelets tipped with animal-head
decorations, like the gilded ram's head

atal sculptures that we
rate important building
e drank from bronze
inted themselves with
stored in glazed jars.

h bulls' horns.

ch out toward the

famous objects in the museum
an intriguing combination of myth,
ory and legend.

prism was mounted on a central
indle so that it could be rotated. It
ts a succession of cities, their rulers
nd the length of their reign going
back to the creation of kingship. The list
does not present a factual history. It's
a literary creation that connects the
current ruler with the god-given gift
of civilisation. Some of the earliest kings
are mythical and alleged to have ruled
for over 20,000 years, while the later
entries increasingly connected
with history.

Find out more about the king list
on the digital kiosk in the front of
this case.

Ruled by an Assyrian prince

stone was one
rick walls of
imrud in

ce these designs
they are all stylised
ts. Look for symmetrical
ons and ibex with
hers have a 'master
ure flanked by wild
grasp by the neck.

Masterpieces of metalwork →

The two pieces at the top are ferocious
looking axe heads, although they have
never been sharpened and so may have
been purely ceremonial.

The pins were probably for clothing –

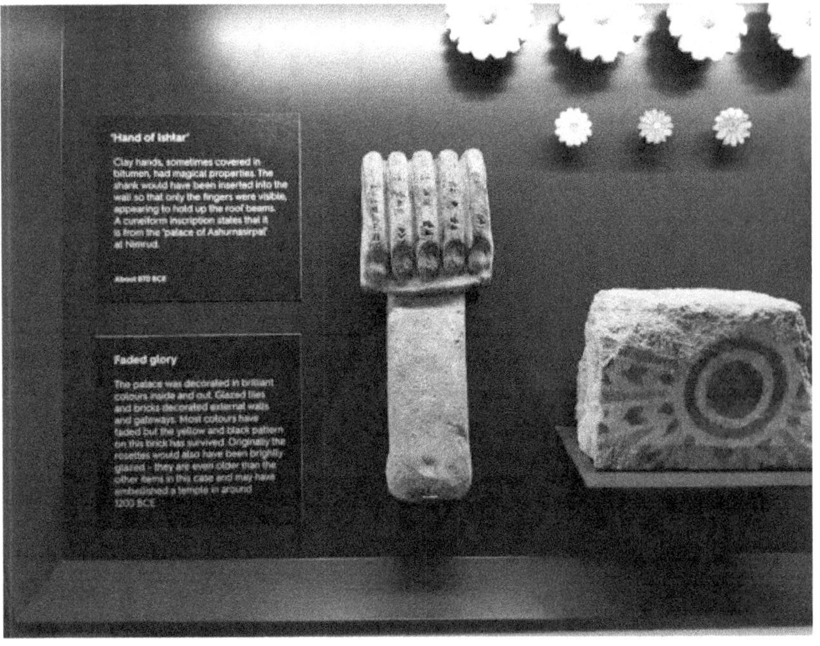
'Hand of Ishtar'

Clay hands, sometimes covered in
bitumen, had magical properties. The
shank would have been inserted into the
wall so that only the fingers were visible,
appearing to hold up the roof beams.
A cuneiform inscription states that it
is from the 'palace of Ashurnasirpal'
at Nimrud.

About 870 BCE

Faded glory

The palace was decorated in brilliant
colours inside and out. Glazed tiles
and bricks decorated external walls
and gateways. Most colours have
faded but the yellow and black pattern
on this brick has survived. Originally the
rosettes would also have been brightly
glazed – they are even older than the
other items in this case and may have
embellished a temple in around
1200 BCE.

'Message from the king of Alashiya...

borrow
bread   To be
to be
but to
sick is j

Brick was crush evil men and
rebirth to just men.

to a temple

Don't miss out!

Visit the website below and you can sign up to receive emails whenever RYAN MOORHEN publishes a new book. There's no charge and no obligation.

https://books2read.com/r/B-A-CIVN-VLBXB

BOOKS 2 READ

Connecting independent readers to independent writers.

Did you love *The Descent of the Sumerian Civilization and the Rise of the Akkadian Empire*? Then you should read *Mythologies of the Ancient World*[1] by RYAN MOORHEN!

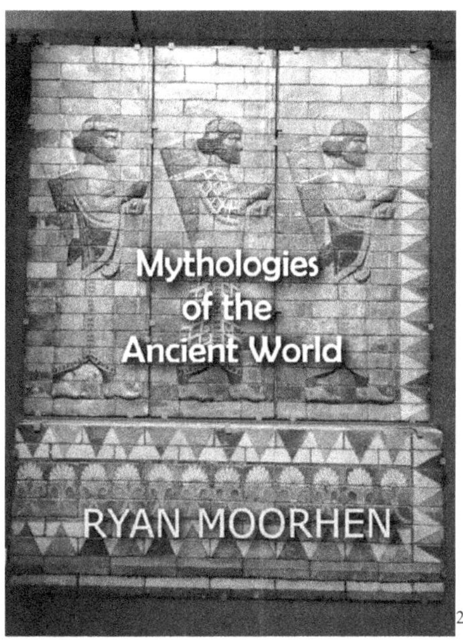

[2]

Sumerian and Akkadian myths tend to focus on the creation of the universe, the origin of the gods, epic stories, ancient sites, and intrigues, and their astronomical achievements and creative building projects for the gods. It is rare for the Sumerian-Akkadian myths to focus on the struggle between the gods for power, and even then, it is not usually depicted as a vicious and God-like struggle. In their theological and cosmological reflection, The Sumer-Akkadian myths show a relatively mature and sophisticated understanding of the god's religious activities.

Many myths are associated with the organization of the universe and its cultural processes, the creation of man, and the establishment

---

1. https://books2read.com/u/3GrRdQ

2. https://books2read.com/u/3GrRdQ

of civilization. It has been found that no Sumerian myth is known that deals with the creation of the universe directly or explicitly; what little is known about Sumerian cosmogonic ideas has been inferred and deduced from laconic statements scattered throughout the literary texts. This myth is populated by relatively few deities: the air-God Enlil, the water-God Enki, the mother goddess Ninhursag (also known as Ninh or Ninmah), the god of the south wind Ninurta, the moon-god Nanna-Sin, the Eridu-god Martu, and above all the goddess Inanna, particularly regarding her unfortunate husband, Dumuzi.

According to "Enlil and the Creation of the Pickax," he was the god who separated Heaven and Earth, brought forth "the seed of the land" from the Earth, fashioned the pickax for agricultural and building purposes, and gave it to the "people of dilmun" (the Sumerians, or perhaps humanity). In the myth "Summer and Winter," Enlil was the god who gave rise to trees and grains, produced abundance and prosperity in "the land," and appointed "Winter" to be "the farmer of the gods," who was in charge of the life-giving waters and all life. His blessing is sought after by all gods, even the most important ones. In one myth, the water-God Enki traveled to Enlil's temple in Nippur after constructing his "sea house" in Eridu to obtain his approval and blessing. Moon-God Nanna-Sin, the astronomy deity of Ur, travels to Nippur with gifts to ensure his domain's prosperity and well-being.

Enlil is the chief of the Sumerian pantheon, but his power is not absolute and unlimited. Enlil's banishment to the Nether World is a story that is among the more "human" and tender of the Sumerian myths.

Read more at https://www.dttvpublications.com/ryanmoorhen.

Also by RYAN MOORHEN

Anunnaki Elder Gods Trilogy
Anunnaki Elder Gods: Architects of the Cosmos
Anunnaki Elder Gods, Knowledge, Power, and the First Order
Anunnaki Elder Gods, Lost Science of Civilization

Standalone
The Popol Vuh Illustrated
The Descent of the Sumerian Civilization and the Rise of the
Akkadian Empire
Akhenaten, the Nephilim God King

Watch for more at https://www.dttvpublications.com/ryanmoorhen.

About the Author

Ryan Moorhen, now identified as a Biblical Archaeologist, Independent Assyriologist, Semitic and Cuneiform manuscripts researcher and enthusiast of all things ancient, made his first visit to the middle-east whilst serving in Iraq. It was during that difficult time he became enthralled in the origins of civilization. Upon his return he embarked on his now long career in Theological Studies, carving his niche in Sumerian Theology and proving the connections between the Sumerian origins of civilization and Theological studies of Worldwide cultures.

Read more at https://www.dttvpublications.com/ryanmoorhen.

About the Publisher

The universe is a vast and mysterious place, full of wonders that are waiting to be explored. From the smallest subatomic particles to the largest structures in the cosmos, there is so much to discover and understand about the universe and our place within it. At TV Quantum Universe, we will delve into the exciting world of space cosmology and explore the incredible discoveries that have been made in recent years. We will discuss the latest theories and models that help us understand the origin, evolution, and fate of the universe, as well as the cutting-edge technologies that are driving the field forward. Join us as we explore the mysteries of the universe and discover the incredible wonders that await us in space cosmology. Whether you're a seasoned cosmologist or just starting to explore the field, this content will take you on a journey of discovery that is sure to leave you in awe of the vastness and complexity of the cosmos.

Read more at https://www.youtube.com/@TVQuantumUniverse.